Celebrating American Holidays

Valentine's Day

Anita Yasuda

www.av2books.com

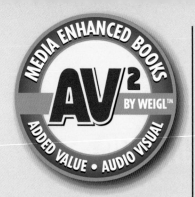

AV² provides enriched content that supplements and complements this book Weigl's AV² books strive to create inspired learning and engage young minds in a total learning experience.

Your AV² Media Enhanced books come alive with...

Audio
Listen to sections of the book read aloud.

Key Words
Study vocabulary, and complete a matching word activity.

Video
Watch informative video clips.

Quizzes
Test your knowledge.

Go to **www.av2books.com**, and enter this book's unique code.

BOOK CODE

F780252

Embedded Weblinks
Gain additional information for research.

Slide Show
View images and captions, and prepare a presentation.

Try This!
Complete activities and hands-on experiments.

... and much, much more!

AV² by Weigl brings you media enhanced books that support active learning.

Published by AV² by Weigl
350 5th Avenue, 59th Floor
New York, NY 10118
Website: www.av2books.com   www.weigl.com

Library of Congress Cataloging-in-Publication Data

Yasuda, Anita.
 Valentine's day / Anita Yasuda.
   p. cm. -- (Celebrating American holidays : arts & crafts)
 ISBN 978-1-61690-678-8 (hardcover : alk. paper) -- ISBN 978-1-61690-684-9 (softcover : alk. paper)
 1. Valentine's Day--Juvenile literature. I. Title.
 GT4925.Y37 2011
 394.2618--dc22
                         2011002424

Printed in the United States of America in North Mankato, Minnesota
1 2 3 4 5 6 7 8 9 0   15 14 13 12 11

062011
WEP37500

Project Coordinator Jordan McGill   **Art Director** Terry Paulhus

Every reasonable effort has been made to trace ownership and to obtain permission to reprint copyright material. The publishers would be pleased to have any errors or omissions brought to their attention so that they may be corrected in subsequent printings.

Photo Credits

Weigl acknowledges Getty Images and Dreamstime as photo suppliers for this title. Craft photos by Madison Helton.

CONTENTS

What is Valentine's Day?

The smell of sweet roses fills the air. Red, pink, and white hearts hang from store windows. It must be Valentine's Day. This holiday is celebrated on February 14th every year.

Valentine's Day celebrates love and friendship. It gives people the opportunity to tell others that they care about them. Valentine's Day is celebrated in many countries. England, the United States, Canada, Australia, and Japan all celebrate Valentine's Day. Each country has its own **customs**, but all celebrate the importance of love.

History of the Holiday

No one knows for certain how Valentine's Day came to be. There are several **legends**. One legend says that more than 2,000 years ago, February 15th was a day for feasting and celebrating in ancient Rome. It was part of a spring festival called Lupercalia. The day before the celebration, girls placed their names in a jar. Boys would then draw a name from the jar. The name they drew would be their partner for the celebrations. Some of these pairings led to marriage.

During the **Middle Ages**, February 14th was thought to be the day that birds started looking for their partner. February became linked to love. People began to exchange **symbols** of their love, such as love notes and flowers.

Make a Collage

Make a collage to show what Valentine's Day means to you.

What You Need

- bristol board
- wrapping paper, old Valentine cards, used magazines and flyers
- white glue
- scissors
- pompoms, beads, glitter, and buttons

4 Easy Steps to Complete Your Collage

1 Look through magazines and flyers to find pictures that relate to Valentine's Day. Cut out any images that appeal to you.

2 Glue the pictures to the bristol board to make a poster. The pictures can be placed any way you like and can overlap.

3 Add glitter and other decorations to make your collage more colorful.

4 Hang your collage on a wall to show your friends and family what Valentine's Day means to you.

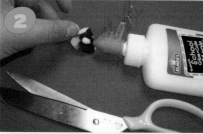

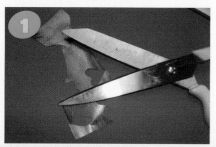

St. Valentine

Valentine's Day is named after St. Valentine. He was given this honor because he stood up for his beliefs. At one time, Rome was ruled by Emperor Claudius II. The emperor found it hard to get people to join his army. The men did not want to leave their families. The emperor canceled all marriage engagements in Rome.

Not everyone was happy with his decision. One of these people was a man named Valentine. He began to marry people secretly. Word of this reached the emperor. Valentine was put in prison. Here, he became friends with the jailkeeper. He helped and taught the jailer's blind daughter. Before he was put to death on February 14, 269 AD, Saint Valentine wrote her a letter. He signed it, "From Your Valentine." The story claims that when the girl saw the letter, she was no longer blind. Centuries later, the Catholic Church made Valentine a saint. It also named February 14th St. Valentine's Day in his honor.

Make a Heart Wreath

Wreaths are often made for decoration to show how much someone is loved.

What You Need

- wire coat hanger
- 16 toilet paper rolls
- red, pink, and white construction paper
- tape
- glue
- scissors
- ribbon

7 Easy Steps to Make Your Wreath

1. Bend the coat hanger to make a circle.

2. With an adult's help, vertically cut a slit halfway through each toilet paper roll.

3. Slide each toilet paper roll onto the hanger through the slit.

4. Cut hearts out from the construction paper. They can be different colors and sizes. You can even glue hearts of different sizes on top of each other.

5. Glue your hearts to the toilet paper rolls. Make sure there are enough hearts to cover the toilet paper rolls.

6. Tie a ribbon to the top of your wreath.

7. Hang it on your front door for others to see.

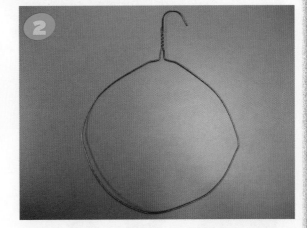

Celebrating Today

Valentine's Day is celebrated on February 14th around the world. Symbols of love and friendship are exchanged. People send each other flowers, chocolates, and other gifts. Billions of Valentine cards are exchanged on this day.

Schools often arrange for students to send Valentines to their classmates. A postbox is placed in the classroom. Students take turns putting their Valentines in them. They are later delivered.

A Button for My Valentine

Small gifts of love and friendship are a Valentine's Day **tradition**. Now you can make your own Valentine's Day gifts and give them to friends or family members.

What You Need

- a large button
- safety pin
- red glitter

- white glue
- scissors
- red pen

6 Easy Steps to Complete Your Button

1. Cut out a piece of paper in the shape of a heart slightly smaller than your button.

2. Use the red pen to write a Valentine's Day phrase, such as "I Love You" or "Be Mine," on the paper.

3. Dab glue around the edges and sprinkle the glitter.

4. Glue the paper to the top of your button, and let dry.

5. Glue the safety pin to the back of the button.

6. When dry, you can wear your creation or give it to a friend.

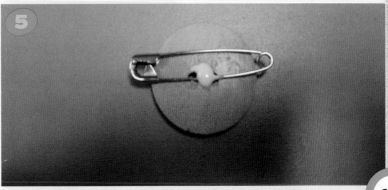

Say It With Flowers

Flowers are a popular gift on Valentine's Day. Many people send their loved ones long-stemmed roses on this day. A rose is a symbol of romance and love. Each rose color has its own meaning. A red rose means love, and a yellow rose means friendship.

In Roman **mythology**, the rose was linked to the god Cupid. In one story, Cupid spills a drop of nectar at Mount Olympus, the home of the gods. A rose then begins to grow on the exact spot. Cupid is also known for his bow and arrows. When people are hit with Cupid's arrow, they are supposed to fall in love.

Make a Pinwheel Bouquet

In this activity, you are going to make three pinwheel flowers.

What You Need

- 9 total, 3-inch (7.5-centimeter) squares of red and pink craft paper or wrapping paper
- pencil
- scissors
- ruler
- pipe cleaner

8 Easy Steps to Complete Your Bouquet

1. Draw a line from the top right corner to the bottom left corner and one from the top left corner to the bottom right corner on each piece of paper.

2. With a pencil, poke a small hole in the corner of each triangular section.

3. Carefully cut along the lines, being certain to stop just before the center where the lines meet.

4. Poke a pipe cleaner through the center.

5. Working counter clockwise, bring each section into the middle. Push the pipe cleaner through each hole.

6. Bend the short end of the pipe cleaner that is poking through the hole to hold the paper together. The pinwheel flower should spin freely without falling off.

7. Make two more pinwheel flowers.

8. Attach a piece of string to tie your bouquet together.

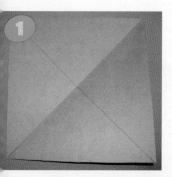

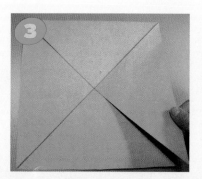

Valentine's Day Cards

Sending cards has been a Valentine's Day tradition for more than 600 years. The first Valentine cards were handmade. People used special colored paper, watercolors, satin, feathers, and lace to make their cards. It took hours to create them. Valentines were thought to be very special and were prized.

In the 1800s, businesses began selling Valentine's Day cards for others to send to their loved ones. Today, most people buy their cards in stores. Some people now send cards over the Internet.

Heart-Stamped Valentine

Give this heart-stamped valentine to special friends.

What You Need

- cereal box
- pencil
- elastic bands
- scissors
- glue
- red and pink paint

- paper plates
- gold-tipped marker
- 8.5 by 11-inch (21-by 28-centimeter) white paper

7 Easy Steps to Complete Your Valentine

1. Cut out one 2-inch (6-centimeter) square from the cereal box. This square will act as the base of a stamp for your Valentine.

2. Draw a Valentine's symbol, such as a heart, on the stamp.

3. Cut pieces of the elastic bands, and glue them inside the drawing. Let the glue dry.

4. Fold the 8.5 by 11-inch (21 by 28-centimeter) white paper in half.

5. Pour each color of paint onto a paper plate. Dip the stamper into the paint, and press firmly onto the paper. By blotting the stamper on a paper towel, you can avoid having excess paint on your Valentine.

6. When the paint on the Valentine has dried, take the gold tipped marker, and add some extra details.

7. Your Valentine is now ready to be given to a friend. You can easily make more several Valentines with the same stamp. You can also add a special Valentine's Day message to your Valentines.

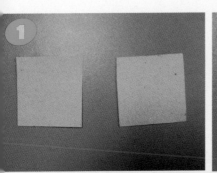

Love Birds

Images of birds have been used on Valentine's Day for hundreds of years. Of all birds, it is doves and lovebirds whose images are most often seen on cards. The dove is a symbol of love and **loyalty**. This is because doves **mate** for life.

Tiny parrots from Africa called lovebirds are another favorite Valentine's Day symbol. Lovebird pairs like to sit close together and are rarely seen apart from one another. They remind people of a couple in love.

Lovebird Letter

For this Valentine's Day, you can make a little bird. It will deliver your Valentine's message.

What You Need

- 1 large and 1 small pompom
- red paper
- orange paper
- wiggly eyes
- scissors
- glue
- red glitter

7 Easy Steps to Complete Your Lovebird

1. Glue the small pompom to the large pompom.

2. Draw two hearts on the red paper for the wings. Cut the hearts out.

3. Dab a bit of glue around the edges of the heart wings, and sprinkle with glitter.

4. While you are waiting for the wings to dry, cut out a small orange triangle for the beak. Apply to the small pompom with glue.

5. Glue the wiggly eyes to the small pompom.

6. Glue the wings to the large pompom.

7. On a narrow piece of white paper, write a Valentine's message. Place it behind one of the wings. Give your lovebird to a friend or family member.

A Song to Remember

On Valentine's Day, thoughts turn to love and romance. Many people use poetry as a way to express these feelings. Some people write special poems for their loved ones. Others buy Valentines that feature romantic poems.

A Red, Red Rose

O my Love's like a red, red rose
That's newly sprung in June;
O my Love's like the melody
That's sweetly play'd in tune.

As fair art thou, my bonnie lass,
So deep in love am I:
And I will love thee still, my dear,
Till a' the seas gang dry:

Till a' the seas gang dry, my dear,

And the rocks melt with the sun:
I will love thee still, my dear,
While the sands o' life shall run.

And fare thee well, my only Love
And fare thee well, a while!
And I will come again, my Love,
Tho' it were ten thousand mile.

-Robert Burns

Write a Poem

Try writing a short Valentine's Day poem. This style of poem is called a diamante. It has seven lines. The finished poem looks like a diamond.

What You Need

Pencil
paper

1 One word. This is the subject of the poem.

2 Two words. Write two adjectives, or descriptive words, that tell about line one.

3 Three words. Write three verbs ending in "ing."

4 Four words. Write four nouns about the poem's subject.

5 Three words. Write three "ing" verbs about the subject.

6 Two words. Write two adjectives that describe line seven.

7 One Word. Write a noun that is the opposite of line one.

Valentine's Foods

Valentine's Day is a sweet holiday. Children bake heart-shaped cookies and decorate them with red sprinkles or icing. People line up at chocolate shops to buy heart-shaped boxes of chocolate. These are often decorated with roses and lace.

Candy is another popular Valentine's Day treat. Some Valentine candies have sweet messages printed on them. In pretty pastel shades of pink, yellow, and mint green, they say "Be Mine" and other Valentine's Day phrases.

Chocolate-dipped Fruit

Here is a simple way of making your own Valentine's Day goodies. This recipe uses a microwave. You will need an adult to help you.

What You Need

- bake sheet
- wax paper
- paper towel
- 1 box of fondue chocolate
- a bowl
- a skewer
- fresh fruits, such as strawberries, mandarin oranges, kiwi, and apple slices

7 **Easy Steps to Make Your Treat**

1. Cover the bake sheet with wax paper, and set to one side.

2. Wash and dry your fruit carefully. Place the fruit on a paper towel to soak up any extra moisture. Otherwise, the chocolate will not stick to the fruit.

3. To melt the chocolate, follow the directions on the box. Make sure the chocolate does not burn.

4. Place a few pieces of fruit on a skewer.

5. Dip the skewer into the chocolate.

6. Place the skewer on the wax paper to let the chocolate harden.

7. Share your chocolate creations with family and friends.

What Have You Learned?

1 What ancient Roman festival is believed to have started Valentine's celebrations?

2 Who was Saint Valentine?

3 What do red roses symbolize?

4 Which god is linked to roses?

5 When did businesses start selling Valentine's Day cards?

6 Why are doves a symbol of love?

7 Which birds besides doves symbolize Valentine's Day?

Answers

1. Lupercalia 2. a priest in ancient Rome 3. love 4. Cupid 5. 1800s 6. They mate for life 7. lovebirds

Glossary

customs: traditions or habits that people always perform

legends: stories handed down from earlier times

loyalty: giving or showing constant support to a person or organization

mate: the male or female of a couple

Middle Ages: end of the 5th century to the early 15th century in Europe

mythology: a body of traditional stories told by people of a certain religion or culture

symbols: objects that stand for something else

tradition: a custom that is passed from generation to generation

Index

Log on to www.av2books.com

AV² by Weigl brings you media enhanced books that support active learning. Go to www.av2books.com, and enter the special code found on page 2 of this book. You will gain access to enriched and enhanced content that supplements and complements this book. Content includes video, audio, web links, quizzes, a slide show, and activities.

Audio
Listen to sections of the book read aloud.

Video
Watch informative video clips.

Embedded Weblinks
Gain additional information for research.

Try This!
Complete activities and hands-on experiments.

WHAT'S ONLINE?

Try This!	Embedded Weblinks	Video	EXTRA FEATURES
Try more fun activities.	Find out more about the history of Valentine's Day.	Watch a video about Valentine's Day.	**Audio** Listen to sections of the book read aloud.
Write a biography about an important person.	Find out more about an important holiday symbol.	Check out another video about Valentine's Day.	**Key Words** Study vocabulary, and complete a matching word activity.
Make another recipe.	Read more information about Valentine's Day.		
Play an interactive activity	Find out about a similar celebration.		**Slide Show** View images and captior and prepare a presentati
			Quizzes Test your knowledge.

AV² was built to bridge the gap between print and digital. We encourage you to tell us what you like and what you want to see in the future.

Sign up to be an AV² Ambassador at www.av2books.com/ambassador.